Uncommon
Minds

Cover photo Credit: Sarah Rollins Photography

Kaegi Publishing
Cynthia Drucker, Publisher, Editor
1121 S Military Trail, Suite #160
Deerfield Beach, Florida   33442
Kaegi Publishing is a self-publishing alternative for first time authors

Uncommon Minds
Autism Poetry, Prose
and Short Stories

CYNTHIA DRUCKER

CONTENTS

Foreward

by Leonora Gregory-Collura

When I was invited to write the 'foreward' to 'Uncommon Minds', I undeniably jumped at the invitation and opportunity. Always a humbling experience, when asked to review a book, a movie, a collection of art, or to write a forward. To be invited into the life and lives of individuals who have brought forth their inner realm for the world to experience is truly an honor and an honor not lightly taken.

Reading this manuscript less than three months away from our 5th annual International Naturally Autistic® People AWARDS, Convention and Festival (now known as WORLD AUTISM FESTIVAL) only further substantiated my passion and commitment to 'showcase' to the world an emerging culture and community, a humanity with innocent values and beliefs encompassing the remarkable core strength held within such a community – a once marginalized group of humans yet to be unveiled and discovered!

It is compilations in books such as 'Uncommon Minds' which enable the demystification of the rampant myths. Myths over decades, if not centuries has disabled the autistic community from engaging with society, to be invisible citizens without 'voice'. Fortunately for people like Cynthia Drucker, and many others like her in our world, the autistic community has opportunity to be supported to shine our light, illuminating the beauty of our vulnerabilities spoken through the written word and visual art as the reader will experience in this book.

After several hours of being drawn into the depth of the fabric of life of each contributor, artist, poet and writer, I was catapulted into my own life, into the depths of a spring's underground, experiencing "the I and the Me" as the flowing water of the spring naturally being risen to the surface of consciousness. The particles of which shared an unfathomed life before me, still yet to discover the 'Uncommon Mind' of my own.

Having completed the book, I was left with a desire to revisit each page and to savour the paintings of colour and hue, texture and rhythm depicted within. A glossary of life brought together by people of varied ages & experiences, and geography of the world. A tapestry so clearly defined by the unique culture of autistic people. I was particularly captivated by the journey I was taken on by each writer, each artist – the naked disclosure of descriptive words, synonyms, character and metaphors, the literary tools painting a landscape from which all may hear, sing, play, dance in collaboration with depicted notes of the orchestration within the pages of this book. A choreography of lives and worlds more common than not! For me, the art captured the essence of the writing and the way in which each piece of art was carefully selected and positioned between the poetry, like a choreography with corps de ballet and the principal dancers and soloists specifically placed, a backdrop for the lines which made up the letters, strung together to form words, phrases and sentences, creating patterns of enlightened colors, the light and shade of which only the reader may reveal.

"Uncommon Minds" is refreshing, liberating and an insightful piece of art. A doorway onto the stage of human experience and emotional expression through the interplay of the autistic universal language!

Leonora Gregory-Collura is a graduate of Elmhurst and the Royal Ballet Schools, UK - Dipl. RBS TTC; President INAPACF - ANCA® World Autism Festival; Co-founder Naturally Autistic® ANCA (ANCA® Consulting Inc. and ANCA® Foundation), author of Anthony's Story, choreographer/producer/director/host of AyAu, ANCA® Radio Shows, ANCA® TV online, co-publisher of Naturally Autistic® magazine, creator of ANCA® BodyTrack™ and international collaborator, advocate for the autistic community.   www.naturallyautistic.com

Uncommon Minds
Autism Poetry, Prose
and Short Stories

What I saw

I left the gym; I had to, because the music made me uncomfortable. I stood by the door.

I waited. I turned toward the door to the gym, and I saw a classmate burst through the door, an aide inches behind him. The aide grabbed a strap on his vest and stopped him cold. The student struggled. Aides thronged at the little windows.

I know what they saw.

They didn't see someone asking to be taken for a walk. They didn't see him begging to have some space.

They saw an escape attempt. A noncompliant escape attempt. A student trying to outsmart the teachers, to get his way.

They saw someone who didn't understand the point of P.E.

They saw a runner.

He pulled away, and the aide pushed him back through the gym door, shouting "In we go! In we go! In we go," his hands pulling and pushing as the student dug his heels in. Everyone else "encouraged" from the sidelines. I saw too much happening.

I saw an apraxic struggle. I saw a nonverbal student being pushed through a door in a frenzy of movement, everyone shouting at the same time, bent over with hands thrusting at his back, pushing against the doorframe and struggling to stay upright. I saw too much, *too much.*

I saw a blur of movement and sounds coming at me from every direction, I saw the ceiling the doorframe the floor somebody's hands everyone shouting. I saw the final thrust through the door, met with bright lights and cheering, everyone applauding the *nice save!* I saw dizzy and disoriented. I saw what he saw.

I saw a classmate who couldn't respond to prompts because they were coming too fast, and who couldn't comply because everything was being thrown at him at once.

He slumped against the gym wall and slammed his head back. The act was met with a sharp reprimand from a bystanding aide. And I know what they saw. They saw defiance. Headbanging behavior. A tantrum. I saw a student trying to block out external input. I *saw*. Everyone else gawked and chattered as the other kids did the warm-ups. I stood by helplessly. I saw a humiliated man sitting against a wall in a corner, helpless and outnumbered, with no way to communicate. I saw what he saw, the flash of students flying all around me and I saw people surrounding me, cheering, *cheering* for the aide as though it was some big victory to drag a student back into a classroom. I saw the world whirling around my head and it hitting the wall just to drown out the noise.

I saw that nobody was asking themselves how he might feel. I didn't just see the defeat, though, the lack of dignity or respect; I saw humiliation. Oh, yes, I saw. *Pain.*

I watched in horror. I felt for him. I felt with him. An aide, concerned that I had left, asked me if I was ok. Then she smiled at me *knowingly.* Chuckled, "He's having a little fit."

No. That's not what I saw.

I saw an overwhelmed student trying to escape a hostile environment. An attempt to find a safe place, or a bathroom, or some water. I saw a hasty and disjointed "rescue" that fried his emotions and ability to think. I saw visual, auditory, vestibular and tactile input slam him like a truck. I saw vestibular upheaval, and I saw desperation and fear and frustration because nobody understood, *not one of them.*

They saw a fit. They didn't see what I saw.

I know, I mouthed across the aisle. *It's ok. I know.* He smiled back at me.*I know.*

The bus engine rumbled, and we began to pull out of the lot. They were still talking about him, imputing motives based on their own experience. I knew that he could hear them. That they didn't really care. That it wasn't my place to correct them. To try and educate them. Not the student's place.

I saw the look on his face, and I knew that nobody understood. He sat alone, leaning against the vinyl of his seat, his expression fraught with distress, his eyebrows knit. I knew that they were fine, and they could sit there and casually theorize about it, but that he was still coming down. I saw the look in his eyes. I didn't know what to say. I saw his hand, resting on the seat. Hesitating, I leaned into the aisle and placed mine next to it. I didn't know how else to say *I support you.*

His thumb wrapped itself around two of my fingers, and for a moment it was like that. Then he lifted his hand and took mine in it. I squeezed. *I know.*

We stayed that way for about a minute. The bus rumbled down the street, curving around the corners, my hand in his.

They said I helped calm him down. Sometimes people underestimate what it means to acknowledge someone's humanity. To see it. I don't know what they thought my gesture was, but we knew what it was. A show of solidarity. A quiet one, not a trumpeting fanfare, but a whisper. *I know.*

This is what I saw. Very different from what the teachers saw. I don't know exactly what he saw. I believe that it was terrifying. But I hope . . . I hope . . . that after the terror . . . I hope that he saw a friend.

KITT MCKENZIE MARTIN
Terrebonne, Oregon USA

The Unspoken

These are my people
their suffering is mine
and their pain is my burden to bear
if I don't speak out.

Autistics,
when I see them abused,
used and reused
their power diffused to a myriad of "like-you's"
they're told if they refuse, they won't have a future
their self-ownership taken and made into obedience
until they can't take anymore
until they lose their cool
burn up their fuse, their ruse of being *like you*
–and then they're accused
of noncompliance.

Therapy is a double-edged sword
I've seen the skills that it can teach–
I've seen the way we can help when we reach,
reach out–
but when we ignore the costs
of stressing "compliance" over "independence"
when we consider
only our own stance
and don't think, "Whose life is being enhanced?
Whose goals are being advanced?"
we get the "you-cant's"

you can't react in a way that's natural to you
you can't decide your own fate,

you can't create your own coping skills
to abate the pressure of processing
to monitor your input,
you can't define yourself

can't time yourself
you can't not look like me
you can't say No.
"No" is the dirtiest word
when you're being taught to agree
to conform
as if your very existence
does harm
unless your alter your way of being
but you can't alter someone's way of seeing

I've seen the classroom where the standard
is *Be as I Am*
"we don't say no in this classroom"
no joke
that's a quote
like the right to disagree
is something that can be revoked.
And I know a dude who has two words to say
yes and *no*
but who only says No
when he's screaming
–like, desperate–
because someone has taught him
that compliance is sacred
No is the unspoken word
Our opinion is the Unspoken
 Most people don't understand
our way of functioning
don't extend their hand
into our domain
It's a two-way street
you have to move, too
to listen to us
like we listen to you

We spend our entire lives functioning
the best we can by your standards
but you, on your side,

learn nothing of ours
Do you know that we are not a disease?
Do you know that our behaviors are not maladjusted?
Do you even know that we have standards and norms?

Our culture is rich,
it's not a set of symptoms
What you see as a "signifier"
we see as communication.
If eye contact makes us uncomfortable,
if we don't need it to communicate,
if it hurts us,
you don't accommodate
you try to "therapy" it out of us
eye contact is good, disability is bad
eye contact is good
disability is bad
eye contact is good
normal is good...
What you call *unsightly,*
our stimming behavior
is our way of saying,"I feel."
Excited, thrilled, anxious, afraid, overwhelmed
a stim is worth a thousand words
but you only have one:
behavior.
behavior must be eliminated.
It doesn't matter if the behavior
is our savior
if it's worthwhile
for us to "de-frag" with a little stim
it's the "like-you" mentality
If we're not like you,
we're not right.
Study our culture, and you'll know how to help us
Your neurology is a sin
Hear the Unspoken
our opinion,
Behavior must be eliminated

Learn why we do what we do
Why is that freak tiptoeing around WalMart with a stuffed animal,
talking to herself?
When we break down
learn how to help us redirect,
don't be circumspect
Normal is good, disability is bad
Don't teach us not to value our opinion
not to have an opinion
Normal is good, normal is good
Don't teach us that *yes* is the sacred word
You teach us to say yes at all costs
but you teach us to say yes to abuse
did you know that you teach us to say yes to rape?
and that owning our body is not okay?
Obey, comply, obey
consider the costs
of stealing independence
I'm not here to say that therapy is bad
I'm not here to destroy ABA
–but good God, you don't like to hear what we say
don't just teach "yes, alright, okay"

because you know you would never teach that to your nondisabled
child

Don't value your opinions, don't have beliefs
Say yes to all "like-you's"
leave your No's unspoken
when you stand up for your rights, you are acting out
it's not okay to be yourself

But that's the norm for teaching Autistics
it's like something from
a futuristic horror movie, 1984
obey, comply, obey, comply, do as you're told, Big Brother
only wants the best for you
even though he's abusing you
But you really want the best for yourself

because it makes you uncomfortable
that we look different
act different
it scares you.

This is our way of being
accept it
–if we hurt someone, teach us to redirect it
yes, everyone has a lot to learn
–but just listen to us
and look inside our minds
instead of pretending there's no way to understand what an
Autistic is thinking
because you're ignoring those of us who are trying to tell you
exactly what it's like
When your "therapies"
and "methods"
cause PTSD,
that's a sign
that it's time
to change the way you treat us
and teach us
and that's the point of this rhyme
To give voice to the Unspoken
the opinion
that we have opinions
 So it's time to work together
we've spent our whole lives
being told to be like you
now listen to us
we'll teach you how to help

we are the answer
the answer is not lost
you just pretend it doesn't exist
Take my hand,
I'll show you Autismland
and together, we'll find unity
for both communities

and answers
for everyone's questions
the Unspoken is this:
Teach us to be our best self,
not our best someone else.

KITT MCKENZIE MARTIN
Terrebonne, Oregon

Even More Further Adventures of The Owl and the Pussy-cat

The owl and the pussy-cat went on a ship.
To a land far away.
They went to New York and had chips and pork.
When they got off they had to pay.

MATTHEW JOSEPH WILLIAMS
(age 10)
Hampshire, UK

St. Joseph's Cathedral
MATTHEW JOSEPH WILLIAMS

A Meeting of Two Minds

She checked her e-mail tentatively for the fourth time that Saturday morning. Although their meeting had already been confirmed, she knew that 'people like them' could change their minds in a moment's notice. But there were no new e-mails. Their meeting was still on. She got dressed, relieved to feel she could wear her favorite holey T-shirt and leave her hair uncombed. Even if he did notice, he would most likely not mind at all. She arrived at the coffee shop early. She wanted to be early so that she could find a suitable table and adjust to the surroundings before Ross arrived. When there are a lot of things going on, she could easily feel over stimulated. It was important to sit down comfortably in a quiet corner on her own and have a cup of tea, before someone else entered her world. She was nervous; it had been several years since they first met. She always felt nervous seeing people, but she felt more nervous when there were long time periods between the meetings. She had not seen Ross for three years. Sometimes it felt easier when she saw the same person every day, it became part of her routine; it was predictable, less anxiety-provoking. It was dead on eleven o' clock. He arrived at the entrance to the coffee shop. He looked just as she'd remembered, possibly slightly older. He was short with a slim-build and brown hair. Just the way he positioned his body when standing looked familiar. She waved at him and he caught her eye. Immediately his eyes set on her location and he strode through the busy coffee shop, ignoring everything around him he was solely focused on reaching her table. "Hi," she said. "Hi" he replied. It was awkward. What was she supposed to do? Shake his hand? Hug him? But then she remembered he was like her, she did not have to wear her mask for him. She could behave exactly how she wanted. She did not want to shake his hand or hug him, so she didn't. She simply left the greeting as "hi". He really hadn't changed. He still had that young, cherubic face and his hair was unusually angled the same way it had been three years ago. His plain white T-shirt was tucked high up inside his trousers. She wondered if his T-shirt was 100% cotton. Did he have to wear clothes that were 100% cotton, same as she? "Thank you for coming here," she said. "Not at all," he replied. "Thank you for agreeing to see me. I wasn't sure you would even reply to my e-mail." They seemed to relax a little after that, lower their barriers, acknowledging they were on the same planet. Ross was not a threat, he was an insider after all. Conversation flowed. Although they spoke a different language to the other people in the coffee shop, their language to one another was the same. Other people would not have been able to understand what they were saying.

Ross had interesting hand movements, she liked watching them. They were able to look in each other's eyes, irregularly but quite comfortably. Parting was easy, there was no pressure or expectation that they would ever meet again. But both of them felt a little bit less lonely that sunny Saturday afternoon.

ALIS ROWE
London, United Kingdom

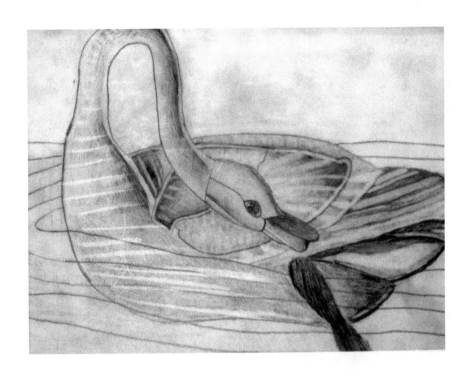

Swan
RACHEL OLIN LEVY
Miami, Florida USA

Penn Station
JAK DAVIES

All the dark places

The light has been fractured
By point of view prisms
Blocked out
By barricades of bureaucracy

Needing a safe haven
In all the dark places
Far from color's prejudice
And tunnel-minded stares

Mechanism of Man to kill the soul
Narcotic news to dull the pain
Sodium arcs and fluorescent flickers
Hide the One True Light

Truth is on the run
And found its safe haven
Let us Invisible Ones join hands
In all the dark places.

BILL BOUTIN
Ohio, USA

Never Touch the Ground

Same words, different views
Same colors, different hues
Same numbers never add up to four
Same players never know the score

Same planet, different worlds
Same lines never being heard
Same eyes never seeing the sky
Same heart never knowing why

When all our lives are laid bare
The truth will be found somewhere, somewhere

Same mind, different thoughts
Same play, different parts
Same mouth never making a sound
Same spirit never touch the ground

When all our lives are laid bare
The truth will be found somewhere, somewhere

Same mind, different thoughts
Same play, different parts
Same mouth never making a sound
Same spirit never touch the ground
Never touch the ground

BILL BOUTIN
Ohio, USA

We Belong to Each Other

I won't always be what you'd want me to be
You won't always see what I'd want you to see

But we belong to each other
And we must help each other
We're all on the same side
And there's no place left to hide

We all need the same, we all bleed the same
We all choose our pain, we all know who's to blame

So we keep on trying even when our dreams are dying
To find that happy ending, we just can't stop pretending

These are tough times, that long uphill climb
You do what you've got to do, no one's looking out for you

Still we belong to each other, and we must help each other
We're all on the same side, and there's no place left to hide

So we keep on trying, even when we dream of dying
No more happy endings, we've got to stop pretending

I won't always be what you'd want me to be
You won't always see what I'd want you to see

But we belong to each other, and we must help each other
We're all on the same side, and there's no place left to hide

BILL BOUTIN
Ohio, USA

Stand up for me

I'm not a little girl anymore
you cannot drag me on the floor
you cannot kick open the door
no, you can't hurt me anymore
and how dare you have the gall
to call me names yet still
when I'm already ill
whence I'm wounded by the lore
but what is it, at the core
which causes me to brood
which starves my brain of the food
it started long before
nearly at the beginning of my time on earth
my character was punched
and in a corner hunched
I sat there capped with a dunce
and told that I was bad
'til it drove me raving mad
and I pseudo-fulfilled your prophecy
and I wandered oh so aimlessly
to prove
just who I really am
whence my right to be, was dismissed as sham
'til I felt like a sham...
you shouted "how dare you ask
for a sandwich
how dare you be hungry
and have needs
to be fed, when you're bothering me so,
you don't have a right to have needs
not a right to be a child
not a right to ask please"
so I gave you my soul
'til you threw me bread
or roses, if I was lucky
I'm was an exhausted marionette

even then
always saying "sorry"
for what I didn't do wrong
until what became my story
was a self-loathing spawn
whence I was told
I was so terrible
a bad egg
from a grand hen
'til I felt just as rotten
and the rottenness spilt through me
as the milk that was spilt
was a heinous crime
'til my heart was broken
so broken from the prime
when my sister left
when she ran away from home
to leave me in your hands
and the new brunt of your plans
to make a new Cinderella hurt
to cover her in dried up dirt
after you built me up again
only to knock me down again
'til my identity was very blurred
not knowing; am I good or bad?
my heart was tossed around in a frying pan
then from the frying pan, to the fire
whence it feels so incredibly dire
whence the background going unsaid
is of a million tears, that were now and then shed
but now, I've had enough
and my anger flows red
as I build my gate and attach a lock
as I vow now to truly
put up the block
that I so graciously ignored
when I tried to keep the peace
while continuing to hoard
whence the deepest pain was stored

and it was to be done away with
I can no longer live, with a myth
of unconditional love
when I know better
so I call on strength
from up above
to grant me the serenity
to set a long overdue boundary
that will finally set me free
and allow me to rebuild
for the hole in my heart to be filled
so I can stand up
for me

ROSE WHITSON-GUEDES AU
Canada

EMILY CHILD
North Yorkshire, England

Black Birds

Alone the boy stood watching the world beneath him moving without even noticing him. Why did this happen to me? I'm not ready for this! Tears were building as he watched the black birds fly gracefully to the small tree on top of the hill. He put his head between his knees and start to sob, "Brother,"□ he said quietly as the flashback start."Don't worry, I'm not going anywhere!" His brother had told him a few hours before when he ran home scared that something had happened. Ok! I love you bro! Hey! I'm going to take a trip to the park. Is that ok? He asked. Yeah of course, but beware the monster that lives in the lake waiting to eat little kids! □ His brother laughed and tickled the little boy's stomach giving him a raspberry. The little boy had laughed and laughed screaming. ˜Uncle! Uncle! Grabbing his shoes and jacket, he ran to the park and climbed the big hill that had a small tree, a favorite place for black birds. Over time they had gotten used to him. Running around trying to catch the cackling birds he yawned and curled up in the trees roots falling right to sleep. Waking up hours later he gasped realizing how late it was. Running home he burst through the trees to see fireman and police in front of his house. Huh? □ He asked confused. A policeman saw the young boy and pointed saying something into a walky-talky. "Hey do you live here?" he asked. The boy shyly nodded his head. "Um, where is brother? Mad and worried I was gone so long! I fell asleep by the blackbird tree. He stopped, seeing the confused look on their faces. Um, where is Brother? The boy asked. The boy started to sob as he remembered how they had broken the news to him. A kind lady came up and sat next to him rocking on her heels. "Little guy? Um, you see? There was this major fire... and well, your brother"...rubbing her head). The boy stepped back shaking his head. "NO! You're lying! I bet brothers waiting for me right now by the black bird tree!" He screamed and raced back not turning around when they yelled at him to wait and stay. "BROTHER? BRO! HERE!"□He called into the dawning night, when no one had come, he fell to his knees and pounded his fists against the trees smooth roots. Hours, he and his brother had stayed dreaming, joking, laughing, now it was all gone. NO! □ He screamed and cried for what felt like hours. The black birds watched him, cackling softly breaking the flashback. Lifting his head from his knees, tears still ran down his face. Sniffling he stands up shaky and watches the moon rise from behind the city line which was clear from the view on the hill. The black birds flying silhouetted against the moons light. Leaving the little boy to wait for his brother to come and say goodbye one last time.

CORAL BROWN
Somerset, New Jersey USA

Fearrow
CORAL BROWN

This One

This one's a
bit player
peripheral
or
tangental to
This one's
a leaner
not in
not out
This one's
unfocused
blurred, less
decipherable
This one's
In need of
a swift kick
some spittle
and finally
gratitude as
This one
pulls focus
away
the others
breathe easier
not me
not us

DAVID SETH SMITH
Virginia Beach, Virginia USA

This Way Blew The Wind

This way blew the wind today!
Just the same as yesterday!
And tomorrow and again…

Through streets and town
On friend and foes.
It matters not to wind you see?
It's time that wind whispers to me-
Time to move on, Forgive and Forget?
There's no time to fill the space between my ears with regret!!!

Every day is a new day
Every day the wind blew this way.

DAVID A. KARASOW
Levittown, Pennsylvania USA

Woman Stretching
DAVID KARASOW

These Emotions Inside of Me

Because of all these emotions inside of me,
 sometimes I wonder what is wrong with me.

It's too hard to explain, but it's more than the brain.
 It takes over your body, most of your control.
Sometimes, I struggle with friends, family and school.
Especially the other kids, who think they're so cool.
If only they knew half of what I'm going through.

If they only knew I have a bridge in my heart.
My feelings walk across it from the start.
Barely any make it across.
It's as if the bridge collapses, and my feelings fall.
Therefore, they don't make it to my brain.

 I don't know what to do, think, feel or say.
Sometimes I just need support and kindness.
I can't take the name calling. It doesn't keep me rising.
 Rising of confidence. But in the end, it's alright, you see.
 Because what I have is my family.

They encourage and support me, and never bring me down.
 And that's why from now on, you won't see me frown.

SARAH ROLLINS
Davie, Florida USA

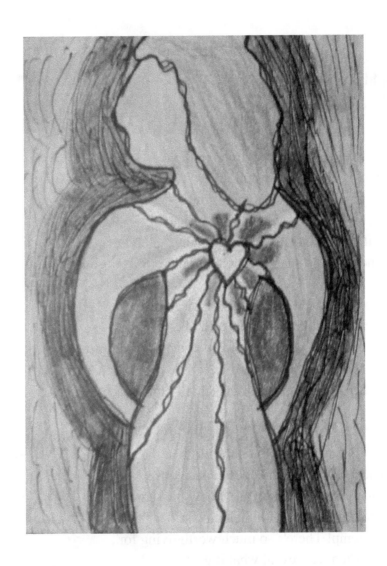

Heart Energy
MARANDA RUSSELL
Dayton, Ohio USA

Xiphias sylvanus

He was a swordfish who lived in the wood -
he couldn't sing or hunt mice
or do anything that the others could,
but with his long snout he could slice
the others' portions; each evening they stood
around him and shared which was nice.

And oft he would talk of this magical place
where he just like all others could be,
and where he'd be moving with ease and with grace
in his element, cheerful and free;
the others would sneer, or they'd tell him to face
the stern reality.

And oft he would stand on the cliffs at the shore,
and he'd watch the wide ocean and pause,
but his sylvan friends would know the score
and hold him back with their claws:
'Don't jump! There's so much worth living for',
but they'd never reveal what it was.

FRANK L. LUDWIG
Sligo, Co.Sligo, Ireland

Stone Age Boy

Karoo sat in the corner
from sunrise until dark,
he banged two stones together
and waited for the spark.

While all the other children
played hide and seek outside,
he didn't feel like seeking
and didn't want to hide.

The adults kept on talking
while sitting in a row
and eating food they'd gathered
from underneath the snow.

His father once went over
and asked the boy: 'What good
is it to play with flint stones
and branches and dry wood?'

'I'm trying to light a fire,
like that after the storm
in which we found the burning
tree branch that kept us warm.'

What makes you think that banging
two stones will light a fire
like thunderstorms are doing?',
the father did enquire.

'I saw it at a rockfall
beside the little pit:
one rock dropped on another,
and a small spark was lit.'

'Good luck', his father told him,
returning to his peers
to whom he told the story:
Karoo could see their sneers.

Karoo sat in the corner
from sunrise until dark,
he banged two stones together
and waited for the spark.

One day he saw a little
bright spark that lit the wood,
and soon the pile was burning
away the way it should.

The others gathered round him,
brought kindling and admired
his patience and his talent
and that he never tired.

Karoo was celebrated
and lauded by the lot:

'Come sit with us, we'll give you
the best of what we've got!'

He said: 'I'm far too busy,
I won't neglect my chore:
we'll need a fire more often,
I need to practice more.'

Karoo sat in the corner
from sunrise until dark,
he banged two stones together
and waited for the spark.

FRANK L. LUDWIG
Sligo, Co.Sligo, Ireland

The Autist's Reception

Columbus left for Asia and was given
a letter to the ruling Khan which had
been written by the ruling Spanish monarchs
but sailed to the Americas instead;
the King and Queen impatiently awaited
the Khan's response and thought they'd been denied:
you see, the Khan had not received their message,
or else he'd have replied.

The angry boss looks at my desk and shudders
and shouts at me: 'Just look at this big mess',
and so I look at it and then continue
my work. As he returns (enraged, I guess),
he screams: 'How come that still you haven't tidied
your desk as you were told? I'll have your hide!'
You see, I may not have received his message,
or else I'd have replied.

With an affectionate smile you sit beside me,
ask my opinion of this little joint,
you ask about my interests and my background:
I answer truthfully and to the point
like in an interview. You give up, thinking
I brush your subtle overtures aside:
you see, I may not have received your message,
or else I'd have replied.

FRANK L. LUDWIG
Sligo, Co.Sligo, Ireland

My Head, My Life, My Me

At times I walk among this life with two separate realities,
The world in my head that only I see
The other happening, it just surrounds me.

Continually pulled by others to surrender,
 to join the surrounding one,
Like I have a choice, so often I wonder which is real.
Could it be my head is wrong or could it be right.

If so then why am I the minority, not the majority,
Maybe the majority have just stopped thinking,
Or just maybe, I think too much.

Is my brain wired differently or do I just access more of it.
Sometimes it's lonely in the minority,
But the majority, In my head I know, it's not where I belong.

So in the minority I shall stay, to hold on and keep me,
For even if just one day I do relent and give in,
Exhausted I become, needing rest, to recover my reality,
my sense, my me.

CILINDA ATKINS
Hervey Bay, QLD. Australia

Teenage Contemplation
CILINDA ATKINS

Alone

Alone at last,
Time to breath,
No more pretending,
Just the real me.

For being alone,
I can relax,
Without the need,
to keep up the act.

Out in the world,
I do not fit.
So at home,
Alone I sit.

CILINDA ATKINS
Hervey Bay, QLD. Australia

Toddler Contemplation
CILINDA ATKINS

Aspie Love

To be alone, is not to be the strongest?
For years I have taken pride in being a hermit ,
the lone wolf is the strong wolf.

Help is for the weak,
always much love to give ,
but always too strong to be loved .

The strength and pride , however, was only shame
and the Jester now dances there over the town square,
juggling towards his own inescapable fate.

When I finally fell, I pretended to stand.
Became a magician , an illusionist
for those who are strong never fall

When the illusion was no longer in time
and the magician's time had past ,
all time ran out.

But when I were to exhale my last breath
something inexplicable happened
and the breath became a screaming cry for help.

A help I always knew did not exist.
A screaming cry over mountains
that had always been too high to be drowned

Longing for an end to the dream ,
I lay down and await my home
the deep quiet sleep.

In a final surprise by life
drums were heard ,
echoing in the back of my mind

Hordes of Love warriors are heard marching.
Their shouts and chants echo in my heart.
- They have come to save me .

He who gave love ,
let love in
and love exploded

People who love unconditionally
were apparently there, just shattered and lost
in the jungles of sheep, shepherds and wolves.

Naked the cynic now stood ,
surrounded by brothers and sisters.
Love warriors !

Together we are strong
and can reverse the storms that whines
and shed all soundness around us.

With our love and forgotten wings,
we can turn the tide and fly
towards the sun and just love.

We might fly too close to the sun and fall ,
but then there are always arms to catch us
and we save each other.

It is our time now,
to become a microcosm
of the ideal future.

JONAS S. LUNDSTRÖM
Bergkvara Sweden

I want to fly

After an infinite number of years,
aimlessly staggering around
on broken crutches,

over far too shiny
and thin ice.
I finally fell into the abyss.

Once fallen,
clinging to false rope,
I could not muster climbing up

I must lower myself deeper,
down into the darkness,

in hope of light.

There in the icy womb,
I lay and torture myself
with everything I have got

On a camp bed firmly anchored
to the bottom of the abyss
with myself loathing as provisional blanket

I burn in the manic flames
of self-hatred, when suddenly
a chemical Shaman lights his flame

The Shaman guides me to an exit
whisper words in my ears
that no one can understand

Blows glitter in my face
that takes me to worlds
no one ever knew existed

Traveling through infinite
levels of dreams
constantly false awakening

Lost I fell between realities
until non no longer existed
and no totem in the world could tell

Like the princess trapped in the tower
longing for someone to slay
the dragon that guards

I had long been longing
for an experience
conveying words
A direct and personal
experience
of that beyond language

Now I have finally formed
a relationship with that
which can not be mentioned

And I just stand here risen
from the ashes of the uterus
with wings ready to grow

I want to fly!

JONAS S. LUNDSTRÖM
Bergkvara Sweden

Innocent

I Love You!

You are fed with the lie
that you are not enough.

But nothing is missing in you.

See yourself in the mirror
and realize that they are lying.

You are just like you are supposed to be.

You're part of something big,
a magnificent creation.

It does not matter what you have done,
there is only forgiveness.

As a brother, I love you
you are me and I am we.

Love yourself by loving me
and you love yourself free.

JONAS S. LUNDSTRÖM
Bergkvara Sweden

Princess Fly

They call us humans
but our arms are wide wings
merely frozen by the breath of icy reason.
Our mind is a bird in its cage
imprisoned behind the relentless bars of rationality
along with language, rationale reason constitutes
the dragon who guards the princess
 captive in the tower waiting for something
that slays the myth of man.

JONAS S. LUNDSTRÖM
Bergkvara Sweden

Dr. Do

For thirteen years I
was pushed around
drugged down and
Seen through goggles
Now they still push but
I Jump around them in giggles
How come you might ask
Well it was no easy task
In the darkest of darkness
he came who did not see less
Talked about this and that
and Orwell saw what I was
and wanted me well
Psychiatry might be a maze
and most doctors bewitched
by big pharmas money haze
and theories of man that Daze
But with men like Dr. Do
Who can perceive outside a box
not only hope for me but for you
I see a pioneer clever as a fox.
I myself am dancing
the Aspie dance
Up down and sideways
In trance for always.

JONAS S. LUNDSTRÖM
Bergkvara Sweden

MAXWELL HICKS
Age 8
Cambridge England

MAXWELL HICKS
Age 8
Cambridge England

Enlightened Living

Life is a trance
every movement a sacred dance
aware of God always
living as he would have me

Love flowing from me for all too see
Thinking of others before myself
always asking my soul; what good can I do?
how can I be of help?
how can I serve?

Answers come in an energy serge
a deep feeling of smile, be good
Live with love, treat others with compassion
all life is a precious monument
to God's grace.

Like the lovely Tejo Mahalaya
it's splendor, look inward
all answers are found there
all the knowledge from forever
time will become a gentle kiss for you
Happiness found within
makes life so much easier
simple pleasures, a smile is a true treasure
dancing with love

I look up at the moon
it's comforting glow soothes my soul
there is no such thing as hopeless
no such thing as impossible
no such thing as alone

God can do all
make any dream real
there is no wound; mental, physical or emotional
he can not heal.

DEVAMBIKA DHAVALAGI

What is normal

What is normal
 Desire, want, need, desperation.
 What is normal
A baby born out of love and want,
 Or a baby born because it was conceived.
 What is normal
 A perfectly healthy body and mind,
 Or a broken body, living a nightmare.
 What is normal
Living in a box, or wandering outside the box
What is normal
Black, white, grey, all the colors of the rainbow
 What is normal
 Perfection, or the pretense of perfection
 What is normal
 Living life Â , or watching life.

LEE-ANN DICKS
Johannesburg, Gauteng, South Africa

My life revealed

As I enter the room, I see the beauty within
I notice the details, the carvings, the art
The moment is joy, love, peace
My heart pounds with excitement

I see a lone chair, awkwardly standing in solitude
A single piece of furniture, all by itself
It is old, used, hidden in a corner
The oddness make me freeze

What is this room, where am I, who lives here
My heart says stay, my mind says go
Fear, love, pain, compassion engulf me
I am touched by the contradiction of the beauty verses the oddness

A room is a place of comfort, a dwelling space
This room allows me to store my life, my secrets, my feelings
It offers protection, sanity, familiarity, a place to hide
I cry because this room is my life revealed.

LEE-ANN DICKS
Johannesburg, Gauteng, South Africa

JENNA WILKINSON
United Kingdom

Autism Love

Autism love conquers the world
Nobody knows what autism love is
 Autism love is complicated
 This is a special kind of love
Autism affects you when you don't know what love means
 What is love all about?
 When you have autism you're hoping that you can make love
 You're hoping that you can hold hands and hug and kiss
 No matter what you have, no matter what you do,
you enjoy the love
 You will learn what love is
Autism love is complicated. They don't think we are smart.
 They don't. But I am.
You will testify one day, you are catching on, you are learning
Autism love
They have it in their hearts; they have it in their heads,
And they know how to love.
 You're falling into her arms and you're falling in love
 Autism love
Love is sincere, your heart is available, and my heart is respectful
Don't get left behind
Autism love.

BRANDON DRUCKER
Fort Lauderdale, Florida USA

Someone Save Me

I lost my way
How do I find my way back home?
How do I decide what is right for me?
How do I change my life?
So that it can be like it used to be.
Someone save me from myself.

What if I choose wrong?
What if I make a mistake?
I fell down so far
And now that I'm back up
I'll keep holding on to the edge
So that I don't fall again
Someone save me from myself.

What happens if I can't fight this feeling?
What if I stop trying?
How do I get away from the edge of this cliff?
How do I walk away from the fear?
Someone save me
Someone save me from myself.

I want to be strong
I want to help myself
But I need someone to save me
Take me away from t he edge
Keep me safe from myself

Don't let me give up
Show me how I fix myself
Tell me how to stop these feelings
Someone save me
Someone save me from myself.

Show me how to be strong
Show me how to fight
Tell me I'll be alright
Please just help
As I don't know how to help myself

Save me, save me,
Save me, save me,
From myself
I just need someone to save me.

IMOGEN ROSE
Cheshire England

Ruth

A light shines within her
She's beautiful inside and out
Even at her worst she's stunning
Because her presence warms my heart.

Her passion intoxicates everyone
You see the world through her eyes
Her moods show you she's not perfect
But even then I love her like she is my air.

Through all my tough times she's been there
She's understood, supported and helped
She takes me out and shares her friends
Thank you, one day I will repay you.

I'm so glad I have you
You made me who I am
I wish I could be half as amazing as you
You're my sister, my best friend, my mother.

I will always love you
I will always appreciate you
I will always thank you
I will always be there for you too.

IMOGEN ROSE
Cheshire England

Our friendship from my view

I help her pack, sitting on her suitcase
We're leaving early in the morning.
The two of us, under the sun.
The rays beat down
Burning her fair skin.
My best friend, my life.

The youngest provokes the volcano, ready to erupt.
Then the larva spills.
When the flow stops, she shakes, she's an earthquake
Saying she is done. Water spills upon her and I am the protective
layer, no harm shall come to the one.
I need my other half.

The volcano becomes a mountain
A snowy white, glorious mountain shimmering under the light.

Sparkling locks of chocolate roll around her face
Allowing the sapphire diamonds to radiate, to brighten
T he faces of the ones she may look upon.
Slender body that will walk with me in step.
I sit in her shadow as she shines.

Her hand comes to pull me out from under her shadow
I am her equal in her sight but from mine she is not just a star,
She is the sun, she provides the light to my world.

A book I love, a book so absorbing that it's painful to put down,
Every day another page is written and every day another page I
read.

This book is everlasting. This book is about friendship, a bond, a love.
Water glistening under the sun hot on a summer's day,
But when winter comes the water turns to ice.
The ice queen may come to visit but on a summer's day she fades away.
For then the sun comes to play I will be there floating on her river,
I ride with her, her flow will never stop.
She may leave but she will always flow within me,
And there she will stay until my dying day.

IMOGEN ROSE
Cheshire England

Dad's Poem

Snake hips Clooney, you can't dance
Oh you must be blind, I'm clearly a professional
Gorgeous George you're not that gorgeous
Oh really because this mirror seems to disagree.

Captain, you fell down a mountain
Oh I'm fine, just a few scratches is all.

Adrian, you have cancer
Oh well, I like a good challenge
Adrian, you just had major surgery
Oh so the perfect time to go for a bike ride then.

You're my hero
Unfortunately even we aren't perfect
All you can do is your best
And that's perfect for me.

Live long and prosper
Live logically and go Vulcan.
I love you Daddy.

IMOGEN ROSE
Cheshire England

Just be the best

You can be the very best,
Than any other of the rest.

If you want to be better than the rest,
Then you got to do well in the test.

Once you are, ace that test,
Then your friends and family might make a fest.

After that huge fest,
You might find a treasure chest.

What is inside of that chest?
Is a very rare golden vest.

Once you wear that awesome vest
You will say to the world,
I am the best!

MICHAEL VIDAL
Pompano Beach, Florida USA

In The Swing
JAYSON HALBERSTADT
West Chester, Pennsylvania USA

The Magnificent Monarch

Oh, wow! It is a magnificent Monarch
Oh, wow! Oh, wow! Oh, wowwy!
Its own blue and grass wings on the back
Floats like an angel on sugar cubes.
The bug shares its beauty with the world,
So the people can stop being cruel.
Oh, my darlings! Oh, my darlings!
Enjoy the beauty and make a change
The magnificent Monarch,
My darling, what a bug it is!

MICHAEL VIDAL
Pompano Beach, Florida USA

Skateboarder
JAYSON HALBERSTADT
West Chester, Pennsylvania USA

WHAT IS AUTISM?

Autism is a genetically-based human neurological variant. The complex set of interrelated characteristics that distinguish autistic neurology from non-autistic neurology is not yet fully understood, but current evidence indicates that the central distinction is that autistic brains are characterized by particularly high levels of synaptic connectivity and responsiveness. This tends to make the autistic individual's subjective experience more intense and chaotic than that of non-autistic individuals: on both the sensorimotor and cognitive levels, the autistic mind tends to register more information, and the impact of each bit of information tends to be both stronger and less predictable.

Autism is a developmental phenomenon, meaning that it begins in utero and has a pervasive influence on development, on multiple levels, throughout the lifespan. Autism produces distinctive, atypical ways of thinking, moving, interaction, and sensory and cognitive processing. One analogy that has often been made is that autistic individuals have a different neurological "operating system" than non-autistic individuals.

According to current estimates, somewhere between one percent and two percent of the world's population is autistic. While the number of individuals diagnosed as autistic has increased continually over the past few decades, evidence suggests that this increase in diagnosis is the result of increased public and professional awareness, rather than an actual increase in the prevalence of autism.

Despite underlying neurological commonalities, autistic individuals are vastly different from one another. Some autistic individuals exhibit exceptional cognitive talents. However, in the context of a society designed around the sensory, cognitive, developmental, and social needs of non-autistic individuals, autistic individuals are almost always disabled to some degree – sometimes quite obviously, and sometimes more subtly.

The realm of social interaction is one context in which autistic individuals tend to consistently be disabled. An autistic child's sensory experience of the world is more intense and chaotic than that of a non-autistic child, and the ongoing task of navigating and integrating that experience thus occupies more of the autistic child's attention and energy. This means the autistic child has less attention and energy available to focus on the subtleties of social interaction. Difficulty meeting the social expectations of non-autistics often results in social rejection, which further compounds social difficulties and impedes social development. For this reason, autism has been frequently misconstrued as being essentially a set of "social and communication deficits," by those who are unaware that the social challenges faced by autistic individuals are just by-products of the intense and chaotic nature of autistic sensory and cognitive experience.

Autism is still widely regarded as a "disorder," but this view has been challenged in recent years by proponents of the neurodiversity model, which holds that autism and other neurocognitive variants are simply part of the natural spectrum of human biodiversity, like variations in ethnicity or sexual orientation (which have also been pathologized in the past). Ultimately, to describe autism as a disorder represents a value judgment rather than a scientific fact.

NICK WALKER
Autistic educator, scholar, speaker, and aikido teacher
Berkeley, California USA

I Am Neurodivergent

Neurodiversity
Neuro
Diversity
Brain
Unique
Whole

My brain is my own
Not less
Not different either
Just mine
I am Neurodivergent and Autistic
Autism colors my brain

It is my identity
As the color of my skin
Is part of who I am
I am Autistic
Not less
Not different either

Just me
Diversity
The colors of life
Neurodiversity
Colorful brains creating life
Enriching the world

Neurodiversity
Brains
Color
Variety
Richness
Whole

Not less
Not different either
Just part of the humanity
Part of the complexity
Of being
Human

AMY SEQUENZIA
Rockledge, Florida USA

Mother

Wings of angels mesmerize
Float above your bed
In my head they hypnotize
Things I should have said
Memories they echo here
Oh mother I hold dear
May your dreams be peaceful
Chase away your fear
Try again
Try again
Stand up and walk
Strength within
Strength within

E.D. STILLETTE
Gordonvillet, Texas USA

Letter home

As you lay there
I cannot sleep
I dream of your waking
An walking home to me
I just wish for one more hour
Till it's all been done
Won't you shake your fists at me
And tell me I'm your son
Leave me dreaming inside my head
Don't be so hard on him
He hasn't done that well before
He always tends to run
Try and hold me try an hold me back
A dream is all I started with
And I'm not going back
My head so heavy
My eyes burn and sting
I am not your burden
I don't know everything
Wishing as an angel does
And seeing only light
I wish I could hold your hand
An you'd come home tonight
Trying hard to hold it in
An wishing for the best
I know that you're looking up
Better than all the rest
Try and see what is before me
Try and live through it
God please take away her pain
And bring her home again

Hang on

To the moment
To the breath of life
To everything that you hold dear
I tried to fall
And I was so good at that
I tried to fall
Never coming back
Now I'm up there
Higher in the air
Dreams of summer
And light
An token kisses, from your youth
Mom and dad
Yes, I love you
No, I'm never coming back ...

E.D. STILLETTE
Gordonvillet, Texas USA

Broken

I tried to steal my life, I tried to run
I went through it all, just trying to have fun
but I know the difference between all right and wrong
sometimes my mind gets blurry though it all
and I drink to be me, and I think that it's not real
and I try to forget about her, sometimes
and I walk another mile, so that I can heal
away from it all
I didn't see it coming, I'd been high for way to long
I thought I had the answer to it all
I was wrong
but now in retrospect, I'm looking at my face , in the mirror
and I don't much like it at all
but I'd dream another mile again, and try to forget
what I've done, where I've come from in it all
I live to be me, that was my only goal
I try an sort it all out, so tired of hearing no
and I will not forget, and I cannot forsake
the times that I life behind me
all the things that I hate
I tried to steal my life, yes just the other day
I'm sure that I'm broken,
 I just hope that I don't stay that way.

E.D. STILLETTE
Gordonvillet, Texas USA

Words

writing once again, just a way to kill my pen
trying hard not to say, what I mean to say
again
its hard sometimes, not to notice
all these things, that go on around me in my head
what do they say, I always hear
I always dream out loud, and walk away
just another, empty rhyme
killing time, waiting for a way to find my way home
tying stones around my feet, so I can swim
makes no sense to me, and come to think
makes no sense, even to them
why not make us perfect, why not let us stray
so many thoughts, of yesterday
I just recognize your smell, the taste of you still lingers in my air
walking slowly, running now
just another way, but not the right way
I know
yes I know
that it all will come to pass
the evil and the good , sand in an hour glass

E.D. STILLETTE
Gordonvillet, Texas USA

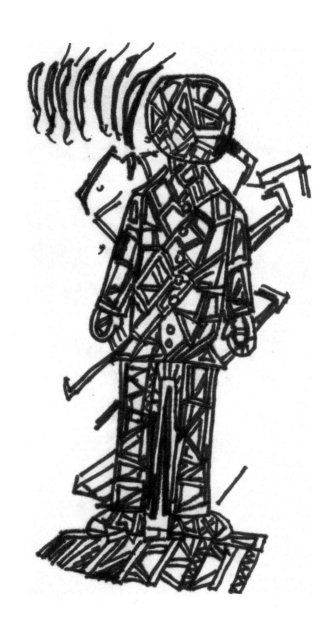

Fragmented body, distorted voice
PAUL ISAACS

Fragmented Face
PAUL ISAACS

The Silence

The silent thoughts in his head
cursing, bewildered, crashing
trying to make sense of what he has
hindered, helpless, people bashing

he floats up in thoughts
things seem irritating
he grows up but yet not
world seems contemplating

revolving, crashed on the pivot of life
he cherishes the inside though
the normal for people is his struggle wide
the simple for others, is his blue

special is what mom tells him he is
yet the specialty feels so wrong

SAURABH MISHRA
Lakhimpur Kheri, Uttarapradesh, India

Cynical

I want to write
a happy poem
about puffy clouds
and sleepy kittens -
but when I look
to the world
for inspiration,
my thoughts always turn
to violence,
injustice,
broken lives
and the weary, knowing eyes
of those who have seen
far too much.
 After that,
clouds and kittens
just don't seem
quite as important.
 But then I reconsider...
maybe the puffy clouds
and the sleepy kittens
are the very things we need
to help us find our way
through the pain.

MARANDA RUSSELL
Dayton, Ohio USA

Stuffed Animals

I wish people
were more like
stuffed animals -
soft, always available
and able to keep secrets -
even the darkest ones.

If you were a
teddy bear,
you wouldn't look at me
and wonder
what went wrong.
You wouldn't judge
or condemn.
You would simply
smile tenderly,
let me hold you
to my chest
and collect my tears
with your plush fur coat.

MARANDA RUSSELL
Dayton, Ohio USA

Timid Tears and Fearless Frowns

Have you ever had
a timid tear
lace its way down
your cheek
and then hide
'neath your ear?

Or tried to
smile - only
to find
a fearless frown
that refuses
to mind?

MARANDA RUSSELL
Dayton, Ohio USA

Poetry is Dead

They say poetry is dead
and maybe it is -
but so what?

Civility is dead
and apparently
so is God.

But you know what?
I always liked the dead -
laying peaceful and quiet.

So all in all,
I think I'll take my chances.

MARANDA RUSSELL
Dayton, Ohio USA

Morning and Evening

Morning is a dog,
greeting the world
with tongue hanging out
and tail wagging.
He is a hunter,
nose to the ground,
rooting around
until he finds the sun.

Meanwhile...

Evening is a cat,
sneaking past town
on midnight haunches
without a sound.
She is a robber,
stealing the light
and hiding it
behind her silky paws.

MARANDA RUSSELL
Dayton, Ohio USA

Facing the storm
MARANDA RUSSELL

Meet the Contributors

Cilinda Atkins was born in 1967 in Ballarat, Victoria, she spent her formative years there until moving to Bundaberg in 2005 and then to Hervey Bay in 2010. It was moving north that rekindled her lifelong passion for art and led her into experimenting with acrylics. After drawing in graphite on and off most of her life (winning a drawing competition at the age of 5), painting was a totally new form of creative expression. Despite this within a few weeks Cilinda was commissioned to produce several large scale works for a display centre in Bundaberg where she was working at the time as a Landscape and Pool Designer. They were very well received and still grace the walls to this day. This positive experience encouraged her to study art at a tertiary level with the aim of making it her career, something she had always contemplated but not pursued for various reasons until that time. With a varied and eclectic work history including everything from taxi driving to landscape designing behind her, she decided to relocate to Hervey Bay where she has since earned her Diploma in Visual Arts, set up her studio and taken the plunge into the very difficult but endlessly rewarding life as a serious full time artist. After the last few years of experimenting with various mediums, Cilinda's professional art practice takes a variety of forms including acrylic painting, graphite drawing, pastels and sculpting. When asked to name her favorite medium. "It depends on the subject matter as to which medium suits it best, all the mediums have their challenges but I enjoy them all enormously".

Cilinda is inspired by the beauty seen in the life surrounding her so the subject matter she chooses is as varied as life itself. She employs both abstract and representational styles in her work which makes this a very colorful, diverse and thought provoking display. Some of her works are already in both private and corporate collections. Since 2010 Cilinda has participated in 8 group exhibitions and won several awards for her pastel, graphite and sculpture work. In 2012 she held her first solo exhibition. http://www.atkinsartworks.com/

Bill Boutin I was seeing a child psychologist when I was ten years old, turns out I had a diagnosis at the time of Borderline Personality Disorder (antisocial) which I didn't find out until years later, so I've had a long and interesting history with mental illness. I was always in trouble as I got picked on a lot by the other kids because they knew they could get to me. My parents and teachers were all very disappointed with my grades not being as good as they should be, especially because I was so smart I was talking and reading at a college level by fourth grade, another thing the kids picked on me for always using "big words." I was in the Navy, but only for two months as I had my first "psychotic break" there and got kicked out. I worked a few dishwashing jobs, then worked at a bakery for a couple years while I taught myself electronics. Finally got work as an electronics technician for a few years until after repeated depressions and hospitalizations I ended up on disability. I married my wife Margaret December 4, 1976, we're still happily married with three kids now grown up. Turns out I have Asperger's syndrome, a form of Autism, and our three children also have it. Robyn, our oldest, died in April 2013 after battling cancer for many years. My second daughter now also has a Bachelor's in Fine Arts in graphic design, has her own freelance business, and our son Matt has a Masters in Environmental Science from the University of Michigan. From 1989 to 1991 I was involved with a theatre troupe in Connecticut known as the Second Step Players which uses the performing arts to educate the community about the myths and realities of mental illness, and to empower survivors through creative self expression in their "Work Hard, Play Hard" program. I have been struggling here in Ohio since around 1995 to start a similar program, Creative Sanity, with limited success as stigma and discrimination are serious problems here, though I have done musical performances, performed some skits, and had been published in local newspapers and appeared on television. The situation for survivors here in Ohio is way beyond tragic as programs have been cut back to almost nothing. I am fortunate to have someone to go to for counseling through my church, many are not so fortunate. I am still struggling, mostly on the internet these days, to write and to continue to educate the community to try and make a positive difference any way I can.

Coral Brown is a writer, artist, and poet. She writes short stories, poetry, and draws anime styled drawings. She taught herself how to draw freehand and has been given tips from some of her artist friends. Her poetry has taken many turns in the time of her writing. She one day hopes to publish some of her poetry and short stories that she has been compiling. Coral was born in Texas but moved to New Jersey at a young age and has lived there ever since. She lives with her mother and step father, seeing her father in Florida or Colorado on vacations. Sometimes Coral is hard at work with volunteering with various organizations. Going to soup kitchens, cleaning up the roads, and doing fundraisers for charity. She is very involved with the youth group at her church as well.

Emily Child I am 14 and I have aspergers, depression, social anxiety . Every day I wake up and have many struggles through the day but my art work let's me escape the world for a few minutes, every piece of my art tells a different story, emotion and struggle for me.

Lee-Ann Dicks I am a mother and a wife. My two beautiful young children both have ADHD, and my son is on the spectrum too. I was born and raised in South Africa, but have also lived in UK and New Zealand. I use writing as an emotional outlet, a way to understand myself and others better.

Jak Davies I am 20 years old and I have autism. I was born and raised in a town called Pembroke Dock which is in Pembrokeshire in Wales in the United Kingdom. My hobbies include drawing and creating art usually black and white sketches of inspirational architecture, my favorite architecture is American landmarks, sky scrapers and monuments, I love all things American I love American history. I was lucky to visit New York City in 2008 and I am still I'm awe of this beautiful city. In my spare time when I'm not drawing I love to design and build cities using Sim City game. My artistic influences include Mc Escher and Stephen Wiltshire. I have always loved to draw. I am passionate about my art. I also love to look at art especially architectural and structural art. I spend a lot of time researching design programs on YouTube to give me more inspiration and ideas for my own art work creations. I am at my happiest when I am drawing.

Brandon Drucker was diagnosed with autism when he was three years old; at the same time he drew his first circle and never left home without his pencil box and paper. His drawings became his communication for many years. His speech slowly evolved and his colored pencil drawings eventually merged into acrylics on canvas. Brandon became an athlete and volunteer with Special Olympics Florida Broward County during his high school years and has received several medals in various sports including alpine skiing. He is a recipient of the 2012 "Yes I Can" award from the Council for Exceptional Children for his ability to teach himself Spanish as a second language. His hobbies include; learning foreign languages, writing stories and lyrics, and collecting DVD movies. He completed a post secondary education, receiving a certificate in Entrepreneurship as part of the first graduating class in 2014 from the Marino Campus in Fort Lauderdale, Florida. He is the author of *Friends of Brennan*, a collection of short stories based on his life, and *The Diary of an Autistic Kid, typical random thoughts of a not so typical kid*. Brandon's art is featured in the book by Debra Hosseini; *The Art of Autism: Shifting Perceptions*. His poetry is often versions of his lyrics and he performs at open mic events in the community. Brandon is a self taught artist. His brightly colored acrylics and watercolors have been featured in magazines, sold in local galleries and art events in the Fort Lauderdale area, and his art has been licensed for products. Brandon's art exemplifies his youthful state of mind and delights the viewer with his bright colors. Brandon's art is often his interpretation of photos and is available as reprints, greeting cards, and metal prints at www.AutismArtGallery.com.

Rose Guedes I am Girl Outside. I'm a charismatic and determined autism, health and social justice activist. I've suffered myself and am speaking out. I'm a young , mom, writer, poet and music artist. I creatively express my unique viewpoints and hard knock experience struggling with obstacles such as; being low income, being misunderstood and discriminated against, healing from trauma, dealing with health challenges, self medicating and challenges associated with the fact that I have Autism and learn differently. Although I'm a battle survivor, I try not to wallow too much. You'll see me, sometimes, having fun, and using my favorite outlets. I'm very passionate about social justice. There is a gross lack of it in the world at this time, but that it is changing and people are speaking out. I am just one of those people. I am also sharing of myself in hopes to help abolish the stereotyping associated with AS and autism. I talk a lot about autism related stuff; but not just that. http://www.girloutside.org/

Jayson Halberstadt is 19 years old. At the age of two he began to draw and never stopped. Several years ago, Jay began taking cartooning lessons from a former Disney animator named Al Baruch. For a young artist, Jay has had many accomplishments. His art has been shown in several community centers, museums, libraries, parks, universities, ArtServe in Fort Lauderdale, Stage 84 in Davie and The SOHO Gallery for Digital Art in NYC. He has donated artwork to several local charities, including a 12" X 12" canvas to the Friendship Circle of Fort Lauderdale and a framed 8.5" X 11" colored pencil drawing to Project Lifesaver, to be auctioned for fundraising. He also donated three 4' X 4' golf targets for the Autism Society of Broward's children's golf program. He collaborated with artist, William Bock to create a public art, ocean-themed picnic table which was donated to the Special Olympics and can be seen outside their office at Nova University. Aside from volunteering for the Young at Art Children's Museum and participating in their Comic Convention for three years in a row, Jay has volunteered as an assistant art teacher at the DPJCC and the Plantation Community Center. He also created a team called Jayson's Giants to raise $1,000 for Autism Speaks and participated in the Inspiration Runway Fashion show to raise funds for the Center for Independent Living. Jay sang the National Anthem, with three other teens, in front of 17,000 people at the 1st Dan Marino WalkAboutAutism. He's been recognized for his community efforts and work in the arts in the Our City Weston and the Weston Lifestyle magazines as well as the Philly Burbs. He was honored as a Powerful Kid semi-finalist by the Chris Evert Children's Hospital and has volunteered at the Joe DiMaggio Children's Hospital, drawing cartoons for young patients. http://jayson-halberstadt.artistwebsites.com/

Maxwell Hicks is 8 years old. I live with my mum and dog Milo. I love cranes at the moment and love to go and look at them and then draw them. I have many crane pictures and like drawing in black ink the best. When I am not drawing cranes I'm thinking about them.

Paul Isaacs is an adult diagnosed with Autism in 2010 and Scotopic Sensitivity Syndrome in 2012 as a young child he was non-verbal and appeared both deaf and blind he didn't gain functional speech between the ages of 7 or 8 years old. He went through mainstream school with misunderstandings and bullying from both students and teachers the same happened during his early years in employment. In 2010 he presented his first speech for a local company called Autism Oxford and currently still works there as a trainer, speaker and consultant in Autism presenting speeches in the UK on a range of topics such as sensory issues, communication profiles, learning profiles, mental health, co-conditions, employment, education and more. Paul has currently

released four books; his autobiography Living Through The Haze, Life Through A Kaleidoscope (about visual processing), A Pocket Size Practical Guide for Parents, Professionals and People on the Autistic Spectrum Foreword by Prof. Tony Attwood & Understanding & Supporting Autistic Students In Specialized Schools. He has also endorsed Jennifer O' Tooles Asperkids Book Not So Average Coloring Book in 2013 and is a part of the Asperkids Advisors of Awesomeness. Here are some examples of feedback from people who have heard Paul speak. "Paul was one of the most inspirational speakers I have heard and all the parents felt the same." "I really feel that all my staff needs to hear him talk. He has such an incredible insight into his own challenges and to be able to vocalize this is so helpful for us as teachers. I would really like Paul to speak to our staff so that they also have the opportunity to learn about the challenges many of our pupils are probably having and are not able to vocalize." "I feel all teachers who are working with young people on the autistic spectrum should gain the experience and knowledge that Paul can offer." His first book "Living Through The Haze" has been widely praised by professionals including Professor Tony Attwood and Dr Michelle Garnett. Paul continues to present speeches, training and consultancy as well as publishing books. This is his message "Do not fear people with Autism, embrace them, Do not spite people with Autism unite them, Do not deny people with Autism accept them for then their abilities will shine".
https://sites.google.com/site/paulisaacscouk/

David A. Karasow What is the Answer? I don't know. I collect questions. My art is my enthusiasm for life. High energy focused past plain abstraction but far and away from realism. This is my self expression, my understanding, my personal experience. An artist since his beginning (born October 9th 1971), David was only recently diagnosed in 2010 with Autism Spectrum-Asperger's Syndrome. David tends to talk quickly, forget fast, miss social ques, talk loudly, and forget quickly and…what? – Oh! "I interrupt others as the ideas form in my head as if in a race with my own memory". "When I talk for very long the target of my conversation tends to allude me" (as does the listening tolerance of others). Still the emotions of a soul usually lost off the map, late, and unprepared, have through art remained true emotionally to the "Positive". "I went through my "unhappy" stage and have come out the other side on purpose and with Purpose". All lifelong David has been complimented as having a great sense of humor and an excellent talent for art. It's as if all the accumulated years of mistakes and sadness due to weak academic performance, poor sense of direction, and social anxiety have been channeled into a great colorful "Hello World". Patience has been learned here, and kindness, and an open mind. David grew up in Elkins Park and Bucks County PA. He currently resides in his parent's basement, but is about to move into an apartment. Although he worked for the U.S. Fed. Gov. for over 10 yrs. 1999-2010 David has remained overall unemployed. David has spent his time in the community by working with groups such as BC Center for Independent Living, Family Services Aces, Jewish Family Services, Jewish Relief Agency, Bristol Career Link/OVR, and Silver Lake Nature Center. David does face painting for over 15 yrs. now thanks to my 2nd mother Connie of Libertae.

Rachel Olin Levy graduated with a B. A. From Alfred University, a four year college specializing in fine arts. She has had several art shows, including one at Gables Gallery Night / Art Basel in Miami, and has published a book review for indiebound.org on Temple Grandin's New York Times best seller Animals Make Us Human. Rachel is currently enrolled in continuing education classes for graphic and web design, and has been working as a private day school library assistant since 2009.

Frank L. Ludwig I was born in Hamburg on in 1964 and have lived in Sligo (Ireland) since 1996. In 1999 I published The Reaper's Valentine, my first poetry collection, have been awarded a scholarship for the Yeats Summer School (where Seamus Heany complimented me on 'a very good feeling for the rhythm and the rhyme') and won my first poetry competition. My poems were published in magazines and anthologies in Ireland, the UK, the US, Switzerland and Germany. As a progressive traditionalist, I took up Poetry where it left off - the Industrial Revolution - and brought it right into the Nuclear Age. I am also an art and landscape photographer, and my work has been exhibited at the Iontas and the North West Artists Exhibition in the Sligo Art Gallery. Being a man in Ireland, I was not able to find work in my vocation for eleven years until 2007 when I became the first male childcare worker in County Sligo. I also serve on the Board of Management of the Sligo School Project. In 2013, at the age of 49, I finally realized that I am on the autistic spectrum. http://franklludwig.com/.

Jonas S Lundström I am 33 years old and I live in a small coast side village in the southern parts of Sweden. I taught myself to read and write and started to write poetry at the age of five. Unfortunately my talents were never fostered and due to family situation and the level of awareness I was never diagnosed but tried to survive. After over 15 years of pain and confusion I started to write again. I am encouraged by the autism community, and this time in English to accompany my new found passion for art. I have no formal training in literature, arts or the English language. Creativity and autism awareness have given me a new life over the course of merely two months. I thank all who spread awareness and pride about autism and help lost sheep like myself find their calling. Endless love. The creative world of Jonas S Lundström www.facebook.com/cwjsl
https://www.poeter.se/Medlem?author_id=28419

Kitt McKenzie Martin was diagnosed with Asperger Syndrome when she was age 8. She is an aspiring writer and a self advocate. Kitt has been passionate about Disability since the age of thirteen. She has been a blogger and Facebook advocate for Disability rights since age sixteen. Kitt spends her free time reading, singing, learning foreign languages and writing novels and poetry. http://autisticchick.blogspot.com/

Saurabh Mishra is a 23 year old guy who is a writer and professionally an engineer, pursuing my graduation in literature. In the mean time, I am warm hearted human of mother earth, not a guy from any country. http://ubergashi.wordpress.com/

Imogen Rose I am a 20 year old girl with Asperger's. I have spent the last three years coming to terms with this as I was only diagnosed at 17. I have always struggled with things and felt I was different. So things started to make sense even though the fact that I had Asperger's made me very angry to begin with. I have left school and no longer want to be in full time education. I have a part time job as a play worker for an after school club for children with Autism. I also co-present a course on Autism Awareness in conjunction with a Speech Therapist, offering a question and answer session during the course. I am hoping this will lead to other things in this field. My interests are film, reading, board games and Comicon. I enjoy writing poetry for myself and my family; my Autism group have encouraged me in this. It would be really great to see myself in print.

Sarah Rollins. I am 23 years and I have Aspergers also known as ASD. I am a photographer who loves nature and pet photography. I graduated from the New York Institute of photography in 2011 and received a two year certificate in photography. I also graduated from The Marino Campus receiving a certificate in Entrepreneurship. I was awarded with 'The Most Creative" certificate while attending the school. I love music and writing poetry. Having Aspergers, I feel that while it is a challenge, it helps me be more creative and think outside the box. When people see my photography or read my poems, I want them to see through

the eyes of someone living with autism and maybe get a glimpse of what it feels like. In the future, I see myself continuing to express myself through photography and poetry and hopefully spreading awareness about autism.
https://www.facebook.com/sarahrollinsphotography

Alis Rowe After my ASD diagnosis, I realized just how much of a need there is to be able to clearly articulate what it's like to have this condition. Most people with an ASD have lots of thoughts and feelings but are unable to express them. I had found little support for females, who often are able to mask their difficulties but become highly stressed as a result. People are able to relate to me, particularly since I have had a very conventional, neurotypical upbringing - for example, my parents are still together, I have one sibling, and I have been to university. Despite this upbringing, I have been very unhappy due to my ASD, especially at school and university. As with many women with ASD I can appear happy and successful on the outside, but feel very unhappy inside. Achievements: Self-published novel at age 20, 1st class chemistry degree and masters, Since August 2013 I have written and published 6 eBooks and two paperbacks, produced branded wristbands and bookmarks, I am a self-taught web developer and internet marketer, I own an internet marketing company, have been featured in the local newspaper, have an article written in a national newsletter, and I am a co-trainer on ASD in adults.
http://thegirlwiththecurlyhair.co.uk/

Maranda Russell is an artist, author, foster parent, spiritual seeker and poet who also happens to have Aspergers. She has been awarded several awards and honors for her writings and artwork. She spends most of her time reading, writing, drawing, hanging out with her family, playing with her five cats, dancing, hiking, visiting museums, browsing local bookstores and doing other fun, nerdy stuff. For more information about her published books or to view her online art gallery, please visit www.marandarussell.com.

David Sanders   I am 36 and have lived most of my life a hermit and undiagnosed. I lived on a family plot with my parents most of my life but have left home twice. I struggled through everything in life including addiction and abuse mostly mental abuse but the finding of myself has been a journey and I would like to thank my friends for helping me finally starting to make sense of it all. I write short stories, poetry and i also paint, abstract. I recently lost my family home to fire and then my father passed away in September 2013 of last year, and I am currently waiting to bury my mother. My life with these disorders has been a long strange journey. a lot of my darker poems reflect the voices that I hear in my head in the night, or uncontrollable thoughts. I'm hoping to have a larger collection of my poems published as well as maybe a few songs as singing seems to be another talent I've picked up .I live in a very small town that greatly misunderstood me most of my life and I'm trying to get somewhere that I will flourish and fit in .. God willing.
https://www.facebook.com/pages/Ed-tilletter/1475797579316172

Amy Sequenzia I am a non-speaking Autistic Activist, writer and poet. I serve on the Board of Directors of AutCom (Autism National Committee) and the Florida Alliance for Assistive Services and Technology (FAAST). I blog for Autism Women's Network and Ollibean.
http://nonspeakingautisticspeaking.blogspot.com/

David Seth Smith I am an autistic poet/photographer/digital artist residing in Anderson, SC. While my mediums are primarily digital art and poetry, I don't favor one over the other. Both form from different processes and express different aspects of things that are often thematically the same, just better expressed in one medium or the other. Others are experiments in style, just visual or verbal interpretations, simple, more direct. This is often an accelerated process for me, I'll first see a fragment that is the seed of the expression, whether it be a simple phrase or a detail in a larger image. Once that initial point is born, the rest is a refinement of the focus, and it is as natural as breath. I hope you find some connection in my work.

http://blognostics.net/blognostics-an-innovative-experience-in-literature-poetry-and-art/2013/10/24/bn-platinum-poetry-lounge-david-seth-smith/

Joseph Michael Vidal Artist, cartoonist, illustrator and graphic designer was born in Arlington Virginia and moved to Florida when he was seven years old. He started drawing at the age of two and was diagnosed with autism at age three. He draws different shapes, logos, ads, books, cards, and many more. Later he was introduced to the computer which became his best toy. Currently he is a student at FAU for his bachelor's degree in Art Studio. He is a proud founding member of ArtistswithAutism.org, enjoying the opportunity to be independent, "Doing what he loves and loving what does." He exhibits his art work at local events. He is the illustrator of two published books: "The Book For your Future" and "Success Express". He is featured in the book; *The Art of Autism, Shifting Perceptions* by Debra Hosseini. But, his big dream is to become a cartoonist, inspired by his mentor and best friend, former Disney animator, Al Baruch. His favorite quote is, *"I may have autism, but autism, will not have me"*. Visit his gallery : www.AutismArtGallery.com

Nick Walker is an Autistic educator, author, speaker, transdisciplinary scholar, activist, parent, and martial arts master. He holds an M.A. in Somatic Psychology and a 6th degree black belt in aikido. He is the founder and chief instructor of Aikido Shusekai, an aikido dojo in Berkeley, California. Nick is a faculty member in the undergraduate Psychology and Liberal Arts programs at Sofia University, and the Interdisciplinary Studies program at California Institute of Integral Studies. He is a leading voice in neurodiversity activism and scholarship, and has been deeply involved in the development of Autistic community and culture since 2003. Nick's blog can be found at neurocosmopolitanism.com, and information on his aikido dojo can be found at aikiarts.com. http://neurocosmopolitanism.com/

Jenna Wilkinson Drawing is essential to my work. I enjoy the freedom and instantaneousness of putting pen to paper. Obsession, repetition, compulsion and patience are not only the foundations to my drawings, they are my drawings. I have an obsession with these drawings, I'm always looking for ways to challenge them and I can't wait to see how the next one will turn out. Repetition is in the rules of the drawing, the rules always stay the same, but the patterns always come out different. Even after drawing this pattern for the past two years, I still have a compulsion to draw more. I like to think of my drawings as my patience on paper.
http://jkwilkinson.co.uk/

Matthew Williams is 11 years old and is a nominee for International Naturally Autistic People Awards Convention & Festival 2014, held in Edinburgh, Scotland. An Artist with Autism who also likes sessions with Riding for Disabled Association and Pony Club (coming fourth out of fourteen in his 1st Regional Show), cooking and eating. He has now also started composing and recently played his first piece, 'Beat song' at his school's music evening on keyboard, with his music tutor playing backing on another keyboard. Website: " Matthew Joseph Williams Art for Sale"
http://fineartamerica.com/art/all/matthew+joseph+williams/all

INDEX

THANK YOU

I give my sincere gratitude and appreciation to the contributors for making *Uncommon Minds* a possibility. Without your generous efforts of sharing your talented works and most personal thoughts, this publication could not exist. It is my hope *Uncommon Minds* will provide further opportunities for you, and help to promote the 'voice' of all Autistics.

Cynthia Drucker
Founder/President
Artists With Autism, Inc
Promoting micro-enterprising for aspiring artists
www.ArtistsWithAutism.org

Director/Events Manager
Fort Lauderdale Aspergers Meetup
A social group for teens and young adults with aspergers
www.meetup.comFTLAspergers

CPSIA information can be obtained
at www.ICGtesting.com
Printed in the USA
BVHW031259261122
652856BV00014B/537